Elephants Don't Eat Spaghetti! © Copyright 2023 Dana Anzalone

All rights reserved. No part of this publication may be reproduced, distributed or transmitted in any form or by any means, including photocopying, recording, or other electronic or mechanical methods, without the prior written permission of the publisher, except in the case of brief quotations embodied in critical reviews and certain other noncommercial uses permitted by copyright law.

Although the author and publisher have made every effort to ensure that the information in this book was correct at press time, the author and publisher do not assume and hereby disclaim any liability to any party for any loss, damage, or disruption caused by errors or omissions, whether such errors or omissions result from negligence, accident, or any other cause.

Adherence to all applicable laws and regulations, including international, federal, state and local governing professional licensing, business practices, advertising, and all other aspects of doing business in the US, Canada or any other jurisdiction is the sole responsibility of the reader and consumer.

Neither the author nor the publisher assumes any responsibility or liability whatsoever on behalf of the consumer or reader of this material. Any perceived slight of any individual or organization is purely unintentional.

The resources in this book are provided for informational purposes only and should not be used to replace the specialized training and professional judgment of a health care or mental health care professional.

Neither the author nor the publisher can be held responsible for the use of the information provided within this book. Please always consult a trained professional before making any decision regarding treatment of yourself or others.

For more information, email dana@anzalone.com.

ISBN: (paperback) 979-8-88759-610-5

ISBN: (ebook) 979-8-88759-611-2

ISBN: (hardcover) 979-8-88759-681-5

For my children ~

CJ and Megan

May you always hold your inner child close to your heart.

With so much love,

~ Mom

Elephants Don't Eat Spaghetti!

Written and Illustrated by
Miss Dana

Have you ever seen an elephant eating spaghetti? Probably not, because everybody knows elephants just don't eat spaghetti. That is, of course, unless you're an elephant like Eddie.

Eddie is a happy elephant who likes everything and everybody. He likes his friends because they laugh a lot, which makes him laugh too. He likes school because he's always learning new things to think about. Eddie thinks a lot.

He also really likes his red high-top sneakers because they make him feel like he can jump very high. Sometimes he imagines they're space shoes, helping him walk on the moon like an astronaut.

Like most elephants, another thing Eddie likes to do is eat. He and his friends enjoy telling each other about the delicious food they bring, and often times they share.

One day the friends were sitting on the playground. They opened their lunch boxes and began showing what they brought.

"Oh, look!" said Birdie. "I have bananas. I love how they taste; they're so pretty and yellow."

Birdie held up her bananas with a smile. Eddie could smell Birdie's bananas and started to grow hungry.

"I have sweet, juicy grapes today," said Gus, showing everyone his green and purple grapes. Eddie's mouth began to water, imagining how tasty the grapes would be.

"Today, I have orange mangos," said Marcie.

"They're sweet and juicy, and orange is my favorite color."

Eddie thought Marcie's mangos looked delicious.

His tummy started to rumble.

"Well, look what I brought!" Ralphie shouted.

"I have crunchy, red radishes. Would anybody like one?"

By the time Ralphie shared his radishes, Eddie was hungrier than ever.

All these foods made Eddie think.

Birdie's bananas, Gus's grapes, Marcie's mangos, and Ralphie's radishes all look so tasty, he thought.

He was excited but waited patiently to tell them what he had. "Today, I brought spaghetti," said Eddie in a cheery voice.

His friends all said, "Spaghetti?" rather loudly.

"Yes," said Eddie. "Spaghetti is my favorite because…"

…But before Eddie could say what he loved about spaghetti, his friends started to laugh. "Eddie, don't be silly," said Birdie in a confident voice.

"Everyone knows elephants don't eat spaghetti."

Eddie peeked inside his lunchbox at the spaghetti that was in there. "They don't?"

"No!" said his friends.

"Oh." he said. Eddie closed his lunchbox and thought some more.

After school, Eddie walked to his favorite thinking place high on a hill and sat under a big chestnut tree. At first, he wondered why tree trunks were hard, but elephant trunks were soft. He looked high up into the branches and wondered how many thoughts the tree kept up there, safe under its leaves. Then he thought about being different and why he was the only elephant who liked spaghetti.

He thought about Birdie's bananas, Gus's grapes, Marcie's mangos, and Ralphie's radishes. He understood why they liked those foods because he liked them too. But not as much as he liked spaghetti.

He remembered when they laughed and said, "Elephants don't eat spaghetti." That made him think even more.

Just then, a chestnut fell from high above and bonked Eddie on the head as if to give him an idea—which it did.

"I know!" Eddie said. "I'll invite my friends over. Yes, that's what I'll do. I'll make them dinner, and they'll try something new!"

And that is precisely what Eddie did. He made their invitations, and they were all delighted to be invited.

Eddie decorated for the party with a tablecloth and flowers.

Ralphie tried to taste a daisy from the bouquet, but Birdie gently pushed his trunk away, saying, "Those are not for dinner, Ralphie."

That made him laugh just a little.

Eddie came in with a giant bowl, and—can you guess what was in it? Spaghetti! It was dripping in delicious red tomato sauce and covered with cheesy sprinkles.

They all looked at the spaghetti and then looked at Eddie.

"But Eddie," said Birdie, this time more gently, "elephants don't eat spaghetti."

Eddie simply smiled and went to work, putting a generous portion on everyone's plate. Birdie could only smile. Ralphie looked at it every which way. Marcie thought it smelled delicious.

Gus poked it with his trunk. "It's so squiggly," he said, rather giggly.

Eddie pushed his fork into the spaghetti and nodded to his friends. They did it too. Everyone swirled and twirled until they all had a big whirl of spaghetti on their forks. Although his friends were a little unsure, when Eddie took a bite, so did they.

At first, the spaghetti felt different from any food they had ever tried. But then they tasted it some more, and what do you suppose they thought about that? They liked it!

When Eddie took another bite, a long piece of spaghetti was hard for him to twirl, so he slurped it up instead. It wiggled and jiggled as it got shorter and shorter, and right before the end, it splashed the tip of his trunk with sauce, and he laughed at himself.

Gus was next to try, then Birdie, Marcie, and Ralphie too, and they all laughed together.

Everybody ate and ate until they all had very full spaghetti bellies.

"Well," said Birdie, with a spaghetti-belly smile. "You were right, Eddie."

"About what?"

"Elephants really do eat spaghetti!" She said.

"We do!" said Eddie with a bigger smile.

"We do!" they all said. And they cheered, "Hurray! Hurray for Eddie's Spaghetti!"

The End.

About the Author

Dana Anzalone has been passionate about writing and creative expression since childhood. She hopes to inspire kids to read more and allow their imaginations to take them on fantastic adventures. During a trip to Thailand in 2021, she visited an elephant sanctuary and met these magnificent creatures up close. That is where the inspiration for Eddie's story was born. When she isn't writing and illustrating, she can be found somewhere in the garden, throwing pottery on the wheel, or combing the seashores of New England for treasure.

www.ingramcontent.com/pod-product-compliance
Lightning Source LLC
Chambersburg PA
CBRC100812010526
44107CB00023B/1271